*Answers About*
# INSECTS

# Answers About
# INSECTS

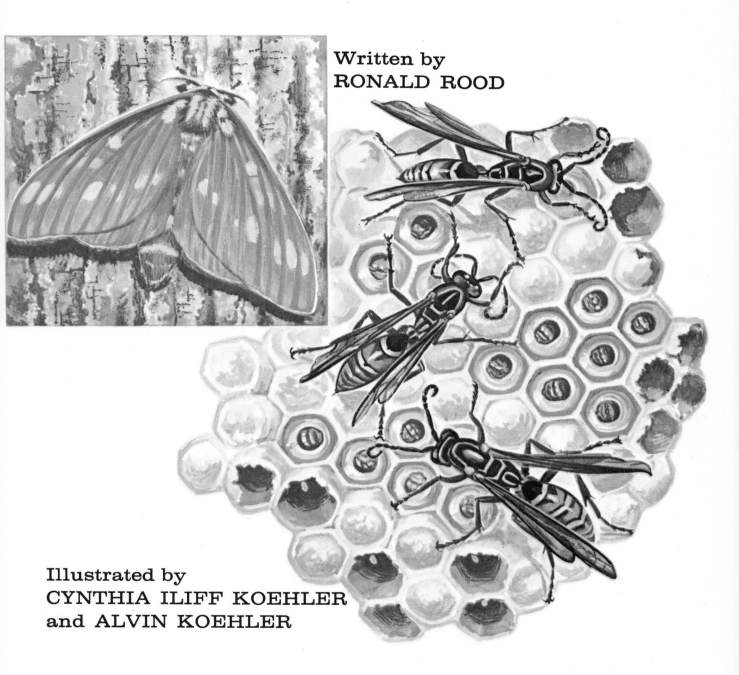

Written by
RONALD ROOD

Illustrated by
CYNTHIA ILIFF KOEHLER
and ALVIN KOEHLER

WONDER BOOKS · NEW YORK
A Division of Grosset & Dunlap, Inc.
A National General Company

Library of Congress Catalog Card Number: 73-86702

# CONTENTS

What is an insect? 8

How do you tell an insect from other animals? 8

What are the three parts of an insect's body? 9

Do all insects fly? 9

How many kinds of insects are there? 10

How do insects use parts of their bodies as tools? 10

What other things do insects use as tools? 11

Where do insects live? 11

What's inside an insect? 12

How do insects breathe? 13

Can insects hear and talk? 14

How many eyes do insects have? 14

How do insects find their way around? 15

What are insect eggs like? 16

Where do insects lay their eggs? 16

What are baby insects like? 19

How do growing insects eat? 20

How do baby insects grow? 20

What kind of homes do baby insects have? 22

How do young insects know what to do? 23

How do baby insects protect themselves? 23

Do some insects hide in plain sight? 25

What is a caterpillar like? 26

What are the caterpillar's enemies? 26

What is molting? 27

What is a pupa? 28

What goes on inside a pupa? 29

Do all insects have a pupa? 30

Do insects "sleep" in winter? 30

Do some insects stay active in the winter? 30

How can an insect help you tell temperature? 31

Are insects helpful to us? 31

Why do bees visit flowers? 32

How are insects used in lanterns? 33

Which insect is which? 33

What is the grasshopper family like? 34

Are the dragon fly family really "darning needles"? 34

What are termites? 35

Are all insects "bugs"? 36

What is the beetle family like? 36

What are the differences between moths and butterflies? 38

Are moths and butterflies different from other insects? 38

What are some of the families of moths and butterflies? 39

What is the fly family like? 43

How do you tell an ant, bee or wasp from other insects? 44

What happens inside the hive? 44

Why are bees important to flowers and plants? 46

How do bees tell each other where the nectar is? 46

How do bees tell directions? 47

How long do bees live? 47

Do all bees live in hives? 48

How do wasps and hornets make paper? 48

How do ants live? 49

What do ants eat? 50

Are there plants that feed on insects? 50

Do some insects live in plants? 51

What is the Mexican Jumping bean? 51

What are fossil insects? 51

What is needed to collect insects? 52

How do I prepare an insect? 54

How do I preserve an insect? 55

Can living insects be kept? 55

How do I make a home for ants? 56

What about displaying an insect collection? 57

Is a magnifying glass useful? 58

Index 59

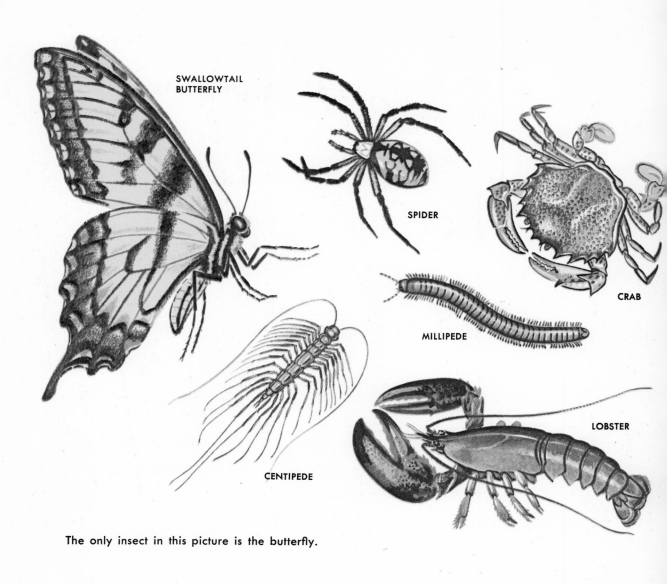

SWALLOWTAIL BUTTERFLY

SPIDER

CRAB

MILLIPEDE

CENTIPEDE

LOBSTER

The only insect in this picture is the butterfly.

## WHAT IS AN INSECT?

An insect is a very small animal without bones. There are three main parts to its body. It has six legs and usually has wings.

## HOW DO YOU TELL AN INSECT FROM OTHER ANIMALS?

Let's look at a good example of an insect — the butterfly. Think of the ways in which the butterfly is different from a spider. First, there are the big wings. Of all the crawling creatures, only insects have wings.

8

Although spiders may sometimes sail through the air at the end of a long, thin, silk thread, like a parachute, no spider can really fly.

Count the number of legs on a butterfly. You'll find that there are six legs. A spider has eight. Crabs and lobsters have ten. Other creatures may have even more. But an insect has just six legs as an adult. Some baby insects seem to have too many legs. Others, like fly maggots, seem to have none at all.

## WHAT ARE THE THREE PARTS OF AN INSECT'S BODY?

Looking at the butterfly, you can see that it has three main body sections:

(1) A head, with the antennae, or "feelers."

(2) A chest or thorax with all the wings and legs.

(3) A tail-section or abdomen.

The spider seems to have only two parts. Crabs seem to have only one. Scorpions and centipedes have many. In fact, the name *insect* comes from a word which means "in sections."

## DO ALL INSECTS FLY?

Fleas, some crickets, and even some beetles and moths cannot fly at all. But they still have the right number of legs and body parts as insects — six legs and three main body sections.

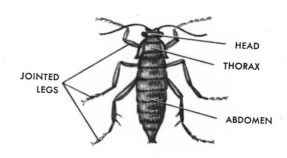

9

# HOW MANY KINDS OF INSECTS ARE THERE?

Nobody knows exactly how many kinds of insects there are, but we are sure that there must be more than a million different kinds. Some scientists think there may be seven or eight million kinds. There are more kinds of insects crawling and swimming and flying around than all the other kinds of animals put together.

Each of these insects has its own interesting story. One kind of wasp makes jugs of mud which bake so hard in the sun that they look like stones. Some ants raise plants in tiny gardens. One fly catches a mosquito and lays its eggs on it. Then when the mosquito bites a person, the fly-maggots drop off and burrow under the person's skin.

There are insects which look like sticks. One of them, the giant walking stick, may be more than a foot long and wider than your finger. It is brown and scaly-looking, like a branch. Its six legs and two antennae look like twigs.

# HOW DO INSECTS USE PARTS OF THEIR BODIES AS TOOLS?

The mole cricket has big feet which look like shovels. Burrowing beetles have shovels on the end of their snouts. They are just right for digging the soil. Water striders have waterproof boots in the form of big legs and feet. These let them run around on top of the water without getting wet. Diving beetles have a little air-pocket. Then they can breathe under water, like a little skindiver.

The praying mantis has spiny legs which open and close like a jack-knife, holding its food tightly. A fly walks upside down on the ceiling because of special pads and hooks which hold it in place. The ichneumon fly has a long drill at the end of its body. With this it can drill deep into a tree trunk to lay its egg in the hole of a wood borer. The tiger beetle has stiff hairs on its feet so it can run over the sand of the beach without slipping.

Bees have combs and brushes on their legs. These help them work with the wax of the hive. They have a basket to carry the pollen from flowers. Wing-hooks keep their front and hind wings hitched together when they fly. These become unhooked when the bee folds its wings.

# WHAT OTHER THINGS DO INSECTS USE AS TOOLS?

One wasp picks up a pebble and uses it to pack the ground on top of its eggs. A certain ant uses its babies just as you would use a tube of glue. The ant picks up its baby and presses it against the edges of a curled leaf. The sticky material from the baby's mouth glues the leaf edges together. The ant lion sometimes throws pebbles up into the air so that an insect may be knocked down into its pit — and eaten.

# WHERE DO INSECTS LIVE?

You can find insects nearly everywhere you look. Mountain climbers find them on high peaks. Explorers bring up blind white crickets from deep caves. Little gray insects called springtails skip about on winter snows. Their dark-colored bodies soak up the warm sunshine and keep them from freezing. Many live inside the stems of weeds in swellings called

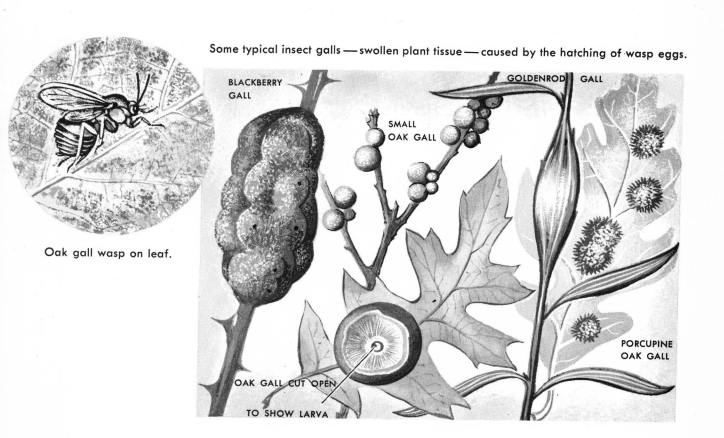

Oak gall wasp on leaf.

Some typical insect galls — swollen plant tissue — caused by the hatching of wasp eggs.

BLACKBERRY GALL

GOLDENROD GALL

SMALL OAK GALL

OAK GALL CUT OPEN TO SHOW LARVA

PORCUPINE OAK GALL

galls. Some fly high into the air, while others spend their lives within a few inches of where they were hatched. If you look at the skin of an orange, you may see some tiny brown scales. These are scale insects, and they don't move at all. Other scales move very little.

Some insects live under rugs and furniture. They may sometimes find their way into your breakfast cereal. Termites and carpenter ants may tunnel through the boards of your house. One little fellow seems to like books. It spends all of its life in libraries.

Insects have never been able to do very well in the seas. Their bodies cannot get used to the salt water. Only a few kinds go into the sea at all and these stay right near shore. So, even though there are millions of insects, they are crowded close together and fenced in by the oceans that surround us.

## WHAT'S INSIDE AN INSECT?

If you cut open an insect, you'd never find any bones, no matter how hard you looked. Its skin is the only skeleton an insect has. Without it, the insect would be soft and helpless. Flies and mosquitos have thin skeletons. The beetle looks like a knight in armor with its thick heavy shell. Even soft aphids live in a thin jacket.

If you wore a space suit that covered your hands and face, how would you be able to feel and smell? You would need little holes to sniff

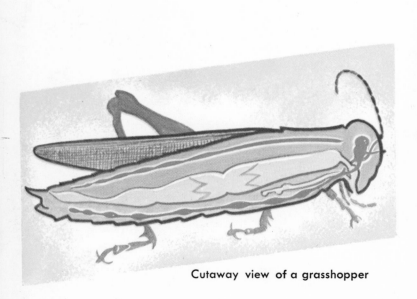

Cutaway view of a grasshopper

INSECT SPIRACLE

Bird taking a dust bath

through, and other holes for your fingers to feel through. Insects have tiny hairs which poke out through the armor. They also have little pits and pockets. These hairs and pockets help them smell and touch and taste.

Sometimes these pockets and hairs are on the legs of the insect. Many of them are on the feelers or antennae. They may be on other parts of the body. So we can say that some insects "smell" with many parts of their bodies, instead of just through a nose. In fact, insects don't even have noses at all.

## HOW DO INSECTS BREATHE?

Look carefully along the sides of a large insect. Your magnifying glass may show you a row of round circles, looking like the portholes of a ship. These are the breathing pores. They are known as spiracles.

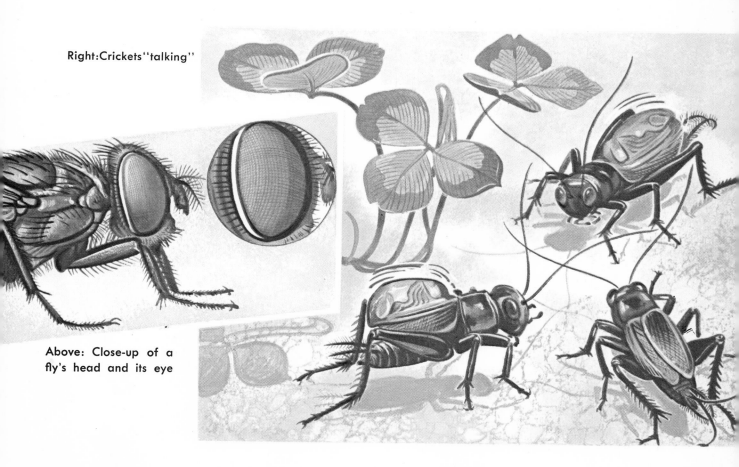

Right: Crickets "talking"

Above: Close-up of a fly's head and its eye

Instead of breathing through noses, as we do, insects breathe through holes in their sides.

The spiracles lead to little tubes. These branch all over the inside of the body, even into the legs and eyes. When the insect moves, air is pumped in and out. Even water insects have these tubes. They get their oxygen from the water around them.

Birds take a dust bath to suffocate insect pests in their feathers. This clogs up the insects' spiracles, and since they cannot breathe, they die.

## CAN INSECTS HEAR AND TALK?

Katydids have little patches on their legs which are sensitive to noise. Grasshoppers have their ears on their abdomen. Some insects can feel sounds or vibrations through their feet, just as you can feel a radio playing by touching it with your fingers. Scientists have not yet found the ears of the champion noisemaker of them all, the cicada. As far as they have been able to discover, it has no ears. It seems to make all that noise for nothing.

Crickets rub their wings together. Grasshoppers rub their legs and wings together. Cicadas have a drum on their bodies. Other insects scratch their bodies or grind their jaws to make a noise. They find each other by following these noises. Sometimes they use the noises to frighten away their enemies.

When insects fly, their wings make a humming sound. Sometimes the muscles of the insect make a hum, as well. The higher the hum, the faster the wings are beating. A buzzing housefly beats its wings twenty thousand times a minute.

## HOW MANY EYES DO INSECTS HAVE?

What appear to be two eyes are really many small ones packed together. They are called facets. There may be more than fifty facets in each of the two large eyes of an ant. One scientist found four thousand in each large eye of a housefly. Some moths and dragonflies may have a total of fifty thousand facets!

For many insects, even this great number does not seem to be enough. They also have a few single eyes right in front of the head. These look like colored beads. They probably help to see things up close, like little magnifying glasses. The big compound eyes help see things farther away.

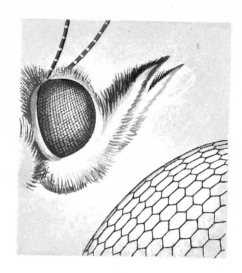

The compound eyes of butterflies and moths are made up of hundreds of six-sided lenses.

## HOW DO INSECTS FIND THEIR WAY AROUND?

Even with all these eyes, insects cannot see too well. They depend mainly on taste and smell. Those little hairs and pits on the body and antennae are very keen. Many male moths have big, feathery antennae which help them find the female in the dark. One scientist found that some moths can find another moth as far as a mile away.

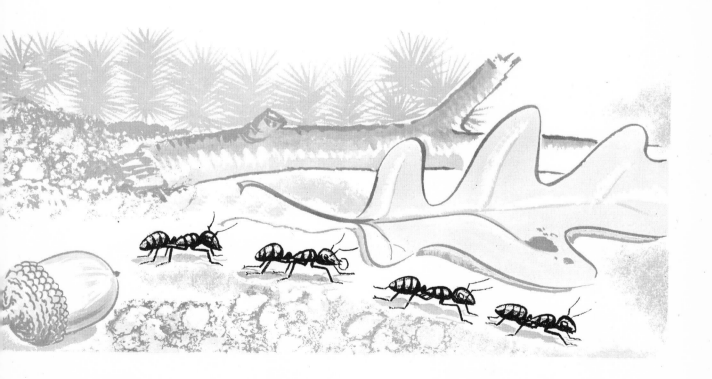

If you have a chance, watch some ants at work. They feel along the ground with their antennae, following definite trails which lead them back to the nest. Each ant follows the trail of the one ahead of it. Now wipe your finger hard across the trail several times. This will brush away much of the scent. Then watch the next ant that comes along. It stops, turns circles, goes from side to side. It seems completely lost, even if the nest is only a few inches away. It may take three or four minutes for it to find its way again.

One scientist saw a long line of caterpillars. Each was following the one ahead of it. The line went over logs and under bushes, like a little train. Then he had an idea. He put some of them on the edge of a glass bowl. Around and around they went, following each other's trail in a circle for days and days. They never stopped or climbed down. They just kept on playing follow-the-leader until the scientist took them off.

## WHAT ARE INSECT EGGS LIKE?

Some eggs are round. Others are flat. Some are brightly colored. Others are wrinkled and brown. Many are black. There are eggs shaped like the crown of a king. Others look like little jugs with pop-up lids. If you have a magnifying glass, you can see various shapes and sizes of insect eggs.

Some tent caterpillar eggs take two years to hatch. Fly eggs may hatch in a few hours. Many eggs laid in the fall will not hatch until spring. Some eggs hatch inside the mother insect, so that tiny insect babies are born.

## WHERE DO INSECTS LAY THEIR EGGS?

Some insect mothers bury their eggs deep in the soil. Grasshoppers poke the end of their bodies down as far as they can reach, and lay eggs in the hole. Some beetles dig down out of sight to lay their eggs. Ants and termites have nests under a stump or in a mound of earth. There the eggs are safely hidden and protected from enemies. Some insects produce a liquid into which they put their eggs. Later, the liquid hardens and the eggs are safe in a covering.

Sometimes you can find insect eggs on leaves and twigs. They may have tough shells so that other insects cannot eat them. They may be covered with wax to protect them from winter winds. Perhaps you have seen the egg case of a praying mantis. This fluffy case is like a blanket in the snow. The eggs are safe inside. You may find a green twig which looks as if someone had been cutting it with a knife. Possibly you will find an insect egg at the bottom of each cut. A cicada makes the

MONARCH EGG ENLARGED

This monarch butterfly hides her eggs under a leaf.

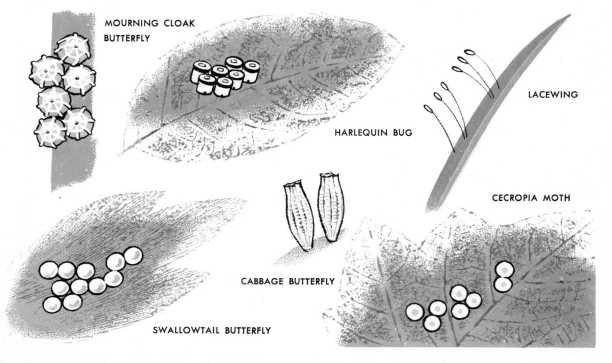

MOURNING CLOAK BUTTERFLY

HARLEQUIN BUG

LACEWING

CECROPIA MOTH

CABBAGE BUTTERFLY

SWALLOWTAIL BUTTERFLY

Insects lay eggs of various shapes, sizes and colors. All the insect eggs pictured here have been enlarged.

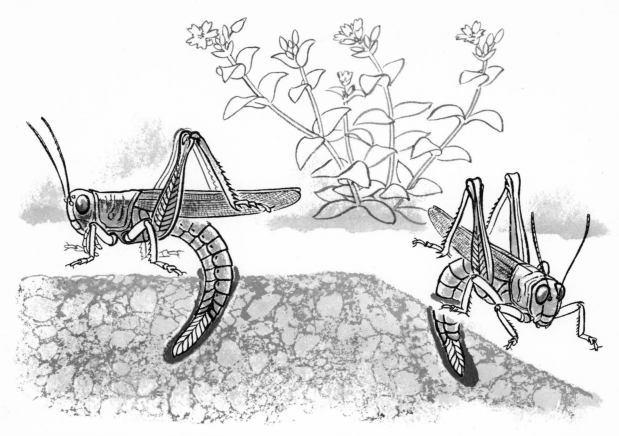

Grasshoppers poke their abdomens into the earth as far down as they can reach to lay from 20 to 100 eggs.

cuts with the sharp tip of its body. Then the eggs are safely hidden under the bark.

There are many other places where you can find the eggs of insects. Flies lay their eggs in garbage. Lice attach their eggs to the hair of animals with a special glue of their own. Some walking-stick insects drop thousands of eggs from the trees. It sounds like falling rain. Clothes moths lay tiny eggs in the wrinkles of coats and suits and other cloth garments.

Mosquitos lay large numbers of eggs on the water. Examine the underside of a water lily leaf. You'll find many kinds of eggs. Perhaps you have seen a dragonfly darting along over a pond. It dips down every few seconds to drop an egg beneath the water. Some damselflies hitch together like a little train. Then the mother fly goes beneath the surface of the water to lay her eggs, while the father fly stays above. When the eggs are laid, the male pulls the female out of the water. One female water bug makes the male bug take care of the eggs. She catches him and lays her eggs on his back!

# WHAT ARE BABY INSECTS LIKE?

Moths and butterflies lay eggs which hatch out into caterpillars. Big, buzzing bumblebees have little grubs for babies. So do beetles and wasps. Fly eggs hatch into maggots. Caterpillars, grubs and maggots are called larvae. Grasshoppers and dragonflies have babies which look a lot like the parents. They have little buds where their wings will grow some day. Their heads seem too big for their bodies. These insect babies are called nymphs.

There is one way in which all these different babies are alike. They are nearly always hungry. They begin to eat soon after they hatch, and keep on eating for most of their lives. So the eggs are laid where the insects will have food as soon as they hatch. Perhaps you have seen a wasp pulling and tugging at a caterpillar that had been stung so that it couldn't move. The wasp will poke it down into a new hole in the soil where she has laid her eggs. The new wasp babies will then have food to eat when they hatch.

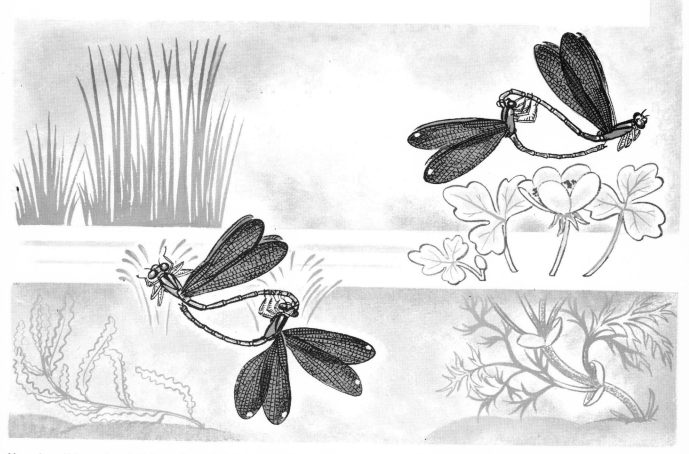

Here is a "damsel train" in action. The female damselfly lays her eggs in the water or else on water plants.

Some new insect babies are so hungry that they will eat anything at all — even their own brothers and sisters. But the lacewing fly has solved this problem. She lays each egg at the end of a long stalk. When the fierce little baby hatches, it drops off the stalk and begins to hunt for food. Its brothers and sisters are safe on their stalks above.

## HOW DO GROWING INSECTS EAT?

Perhaps you have heard a scratching sound coming from a wood pile in the forest. It may have been a family of wood borers, a kind of beetle grub. You can often hear them chewing away.

Maybe you have read about locusts that attacked crops in ancient times or in more recent years. Millions of locusts eating a field of grain can be heard some distance away. They sound like the wind in dry leaves.

A cricket or beetle grub chews its food. But some insects sip their food quietly through a long tube. They drink the sap of plants or the blood of animals. If you look where their mouth should be, all you see is a long pointed tube. Think how it must be to go around with your mouth shut tight and just a straw sticking out!

Many growing insects eat much more than their mother and father eat together. They may eat more than their own weight in food each day. They are growing so fast that they never seem to get enough food.

## HOW DO BABY INSECTS GROW?

The baby insects keep on eating and growing. But they don't grow just as we do. An insect's skin doesn't stretch to make more room. It becomes tighter and tighter, like last year's jacket. One day it splits along the back, and the young insect crawls out of its old skin. Its new skin is soft and thin, and its body swells up quickly. Soon the new skin hardens. Then the insect can no longer grow until after it splits its jacket again. Only young insects can grow in this way. When the caterpillar turns into a moth, or the grub becomes a beetle, they will never shed their skin again. They stay the same size for the rest of their lives. Little moths don't become big moths, nor little flies big ones.

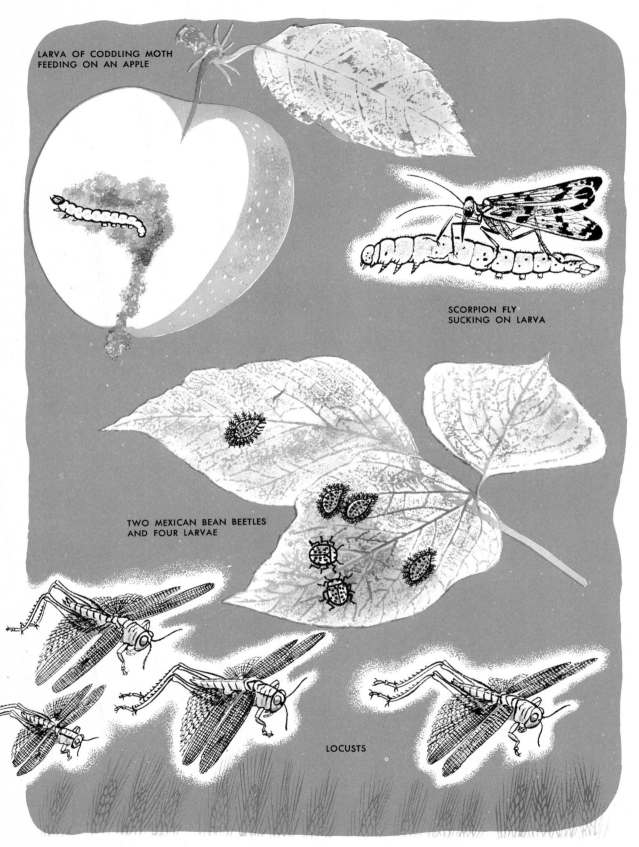

LARVA OF CODDLING MOTH
FEEDING ON AN APPLE

SCORPION FLY
SUCKING ON LARVA

TWO MEXICAN BEAN BEETLES
AND FOUR LARVAE

LOCUSTS

Insects are big eaters. Not only do they feed upon plants, fruit and other insects, but they also feed on woolens, leather, fur, furniture and even books. Locusts are great crop destroyers. Fortunately, birds feed upon them.

# WHAT KIND OF HOMES DO BABY INSECTS HAVE?

Most insect babies have no parents to take care of them. The adult insects usually die soon after the eggs are laid. Wasps, bees, ants and termites, however, take good care of their children. They build nests with many caves and tunnels. Here they have rooms that may be compared to our nurseries, kitchens and storehouses. These nests may be many feet high, and some are twice as tall as a man.

Many baby insects build homes of their own. The caddisfly larva lives on the bottom of streams and ponds. It makes a tube of sticks or sand grains glued together. Then it fits itself inside the tube. It looks like a little turtle as it bumps along the bottom of

POTTER WASP

FROGHOPPER

ANT LION (adult)

ANT LION (larva)

Insects build nests of many shapes and materials. The ant lion larva below waits for its dinner in a sand

a stream. One of the strangest homes is the bubble house of the froghopper. You can see many of these nests on grass blades and weeds. If you poke inside the bubbles, you will find a little green froghopper. Put it on a new blade of grass and it will begin to blow bubbles until it is hidden.

The ant lion makes a pit in the dry sand. It waits at the bottom of the pit with its pincers open wide. If an ant stumbles into the pit, the ant lion has its dinner. Some caterpillars make webs to protect themselves. Other insect babies roll up leaves or cover themselves with dust. Some tiny insects even tunnel in the leaf of a tree, leaving strange marks. Once people thought that the trails of the leaf miners were the writings of ghosts.

## HOW DO YOUNG INSECTS KNOW WHAT TO DO?

We have to learn to nail boards together, but insects can make perfect homes on the first try. Our parents help us decide what food to eat, but most insects usually never see their parents. The hungry babies know what to eat as soon as they hatch. They know how to hide their eggs, and keep out of danger. They can do these things because of what we call "instinct." This usually helps the insect meet all its problems. Instinct tells a Japanese beetle to drop to the ground out of sight the minute you touch its twig. Instinct tells a bombardier beetle to wave its abdomen in the air and squirt you with a bad-smelling spray, like a little skunk. Instinct helps a squash bug put its eggs where they will be hidden, and yet near the best food. Instinct is some kind of inner knowledge that helps the insect to do something, although the insect has never been shown how to do it. So instinct may be described as built-in or ready-made knowledge. Scientists, however, don't know what causes it, or how it was made.

## HOW DO BABY INSECTS PROTECT THEMSELVES?

New baby insects can protect themselves, even in a world filled with hungry enemies. Many of them are the same color as the leaves they eat, so that they are hard to see. Some have fierce-looking spots which make

The Viceroy (right) looks like the Monarch (left).

YELLOW BANDED UNDERWING RESEMBLING BARK

HORNET MOTH

The underside of the Dead Leaf butterfly is difficult to distinguish from a dead leaf.

them seem to have great round eyes. Some have sharp spines, making them look like tiny cactus plants. One insect puts out a pair of bad-smelling horns when it is in danger. Some insects are long and brown and look just like a twig. Others are round and gray like a pebble. Sharp-jawed ones may pinch you if you bother them. Others curl up and drop into the grass at the slightest touch. Still others are poisonous. Their enemies soon learn not to eat them. Baby insects find protection in their shapes, colors, odors, body poisons and fierce looks.

24

# DO SOME INSECTS HIDE IN PLAIN SIGHT?

Have you ever chased a bright orange butterfly in the woods? Its colors may be seen many yards away. Just when you think you have it, it disappears. No matter how hard you look, you can't find it. Then it suddenly flies up from right under your feet. If you catch it, then you know why it has been so hard to see. Its wings are the color of a dead leaf on the underside. When it folds its wings, the underside is all that shows. It looks like an old brown leaf.

Many moths can hide in plain sight on the trunk of a tree. Their speckled color is just like that of the bark. A long-legged water bug looks like a floating wisp of hay. Some green insects are shaped just like leaves, while others look like flowers.

The Cloudless Sulphur looks very much like the yellow flowers on which it feeds.

Resting by day, the Clouded Locust hides its bright-colored underwings under its upper wings, which resemble the bark of locust trees.

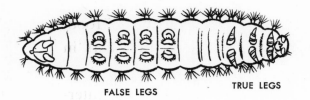

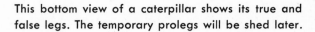
This bottom view of a caterpillar shows its true and
false legs. The temporary prolegs will be shed later.

FALSE LEGS  TRUE LEGS

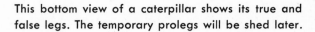
This bottom view of a caterpillar shows its true and
false legs. The temporary prolegs will be shed later.

## WHAT IS A CATERPILLAR LIKE?

A caterpillar's body is divided into thirteen ringlike parts (segments).
Attached to the three segments nearest the head, in the thorax body
section, the caterpillar has six little, stubby legs. It also has a few extra
pairs of legs along the sides of the segments which make up the abdomen
body section. These false legs, called prolegs, are temporary and the
caterpillar will shed them along with the last skin. The caterpillar is
always hungry, and eats almost all day and all night. It needs a great
deal of food because it is growing so fast. So it keeps munching on the
turnips and radishes in the garden. If the caterpillar has to go without
food for more than a few hours it will starve.

## WHAT ARE
## THE CATERPILLAR'S
## ENEMIES?

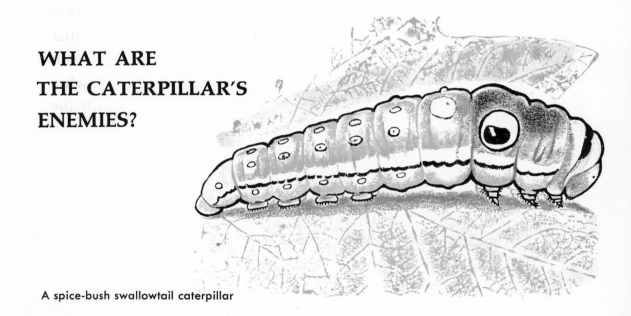

A spice-bush swallowtail caterpillar

When the caterpillar eats leaves that have been sprayed with a
poisonous chemical, the poison may kill it. At least, the poisonous
chemical will cause it to move away. The caterpillar has been in danger
ever since its butterfly-mother first laid her eggs. No matter how carefully

26

the eggs are hidden, other insects come along looking for tiny bits of food, and often find them. Storms and cold weather kill many caterpillars in the eggs, too.

When the egg hatches, insects and spiders are waiting for the caterpillar's appearance. Birds look at every leaf and twig, eating every caterpillar they can find. Snakes, lizards, toads and frogs catch more of them. And when you go out in the field to make an insect collection, you will catch some, too.

Look at the head of the next caterpillar you find. It seems to have two great round eyes in front, but they're not eyes at all. The real eyes are little pinpoint dots which can hardly be seen. It can see only a few inches ahead. Probably the only way the caterpillar knows danger is near is when the leaf shakes as a bird lands near it, or when it smells the scent of a nearby enemy.

## WHAT IS MOLTING?

Like other insects, the caterpillar's skin doesn't grow as the rest of its body does. It remains the same size so that, finally, the tight skin splits. The caterpillar then sheds its skin by wriggling out, a process that is called "molting." But underneath is another skin. The caterpillar will outgrow this one, too. In fact, it will molt several times until it reaches the end of the caterpillar stage, and is fully grown. After it molts for the last time, the caterpillar becomes a pupa.

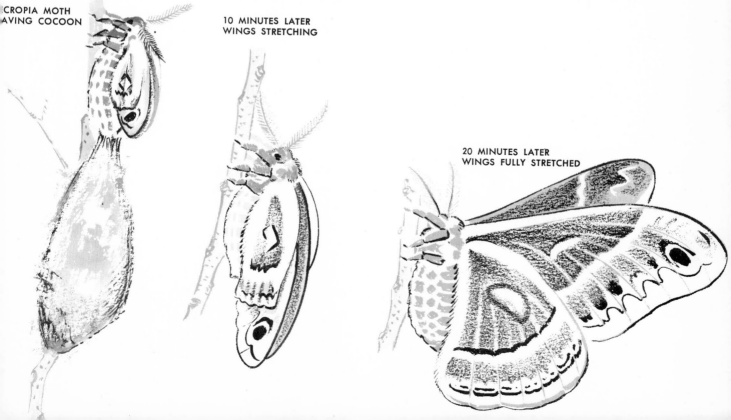

CROPIA MOTH
AVING COCOON

10 MINUTES LATER
WINGS STRETCHING

20 MINUTES LATER
WINGS FULLY STRETCHED

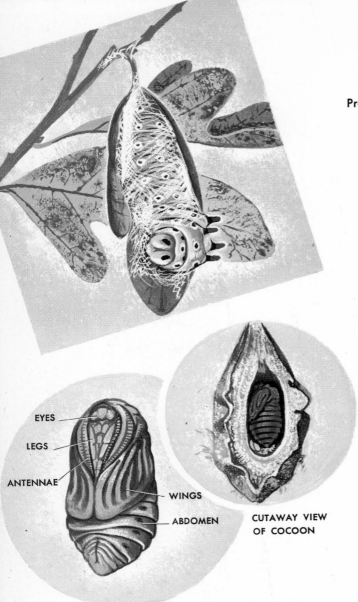

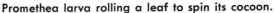
Promethea larva rolling a leaf to spin its cocoon.

EYES

LEGS

ANTENNAE

WINGS

ABDOMEN

CUTAWAY VIEW
OF COCOON

# WHAT IS A PUPA?

This is the stage when the caterpillar goes down into a hole in the earth, or attaches itself to a leaf on a tree. Sometimes it spins silk threads about itself until it looks like a bit of fluff. This is called a cocoon, the name most people use when they refer to the pupal stage. Maybe you can find a pupa if you look under old boards, leaves or stones.

You'd think it would be safe in the hard pupal shell. But mice nip at pupas with their sharp teeth. Skunks and raccoons dig them up. Even big, shuffling bears tear old stumps and logs apart until they find them.

Finally the great day comes when the pupal stage is over. For some insects, it is only a few weeks, but for most insects, the pupal stage usually lasts the whole winter. Then, in the spring, the pupal shell cracks open and out crawls the insect. It is no longer a caterpillar, however. Now it is a moth, or a butterfly with shining wings. The butterfly spreads its wings to dry in the sunshine. Then it flies away, leaving the pupal shell behind.

The parasitic wasp egg has developed inside the pupa of a butterfly and now hatches.

## WHAT GOES ON INSIDE
## A PUPA?

It's hard to know just what it will be when it hatches. But if your eyes are sharp, you'll see wrinkles and folds where the new wings will be. You can find the eyes, the mouth and the legs. But unless you see it twist or turn, it seems more dead than alive.

Inside the pupa, there's a wonderful change taking place. Instead of stubby little baby legs, there are the strong new legs of the adult. Folded wings are waiting to spread in the sun. Big round eyes and long antennae are getting ready to help it find its way in the world. The head, mouth and body are all different. No matter how hard you looked inside a pupa, you couldn't find the caterpillar or grub any more.

Some insects anchor the pupa in place with a strong thread. Then, when they pull themselves out later, the old brown shell will stay in place. Other insects seem to do as well without an anchor. Some black flies anchor the pupa under water. They also have a little bubble. When they break out of the pupal case, they ride to the surface in the bubble. When the bubble bursts they fly away.

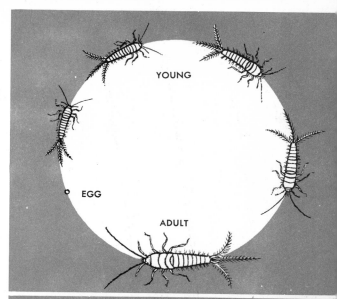

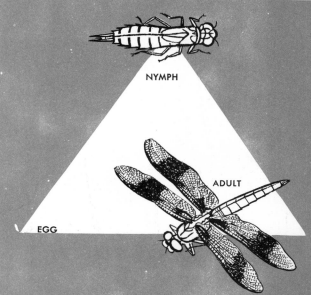

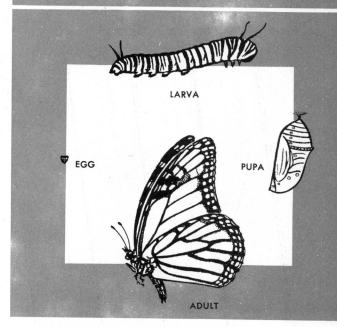

## DO ALL INSECTS HAVE A PUPA?

Most do, but not those which hatch out of their eggs looking like their parents. Praying mantis nymphs change slowly until they become adults. So do cockroach and squash bug nymphs. Each time they split their skin and grow a new one, they look more like the adult, so they do not need any pupal stage.

## DO INSECTS "SLEEP" IN WINTER?

In the winter, the insects hidden in the ground and under the bark of trees are just about as cold as the snow. They are so cold that they can hardly move at all. In the summer, they are nearly as hot as the sunshine. Then they run and fly very quickly. You might think that because insects get so cold in winter, you would want to bring them all in by the fire where it is warm. But if they were kept alive and active in a warm house they would starve to death without any food. So it is better that they spend the winter months outdoors. There they just remain quiet until spring comes again.

Sometimes they come out on a warm day. Then you see flies buzzing around the sunny side of a house. Sometimes you see caterpillars crawling slowly on the bark of trees. The mourning cloak butterfly often comes out on a sunny January day. It looks quite out of place sailing over the patches of snow. Insects may spend the winter as a pupa or larva. Other insects lay their eggs during late summer and then die. The only thing that keeps them from dying out completely is the cluster of eggs. Like tiny seeds, they wait for spring. Then, sure enough, they hatch out. They grow up to be just like the parents they never saw.

## DO SOME INSECTS STAY ACTIVE IN THE WINTER?

A few insects are active all year, even where the winters are cold. Lice and fleas which live on birds and animals keep warm in the thick fur and feathers. Cave insects crawl around as usual, for the temperature hardly changes at all inside a cave.

Even on a winter day when the temperature is far below zero, and snow and ice are everywhere, bees are active in their hives. If you should visit an apiary (a place where bees are kept) on a winter day, put your ear against a beehive and listen. You will hear a faint humming sound. Inside the hive, even on a cold day, bees move around slowly, buzzing their wings. This activity keeps them warm enough so that they won't freeze. A warm beehive sometimes attracts mice and other animals. If a mouse finds the hive, it may eat some of the honey the bees have stored for food. It may build its nest in front of the entrance so that the bees cannot get out in the spring.

A few insects go south in the winter, just as the birds do. The big orange-and-black monarch butterfly may travel from Canada to Mexico. It goes in flocks of thousands. Sometimes it crosses many miles of water over the Great Lakes and the Gulf of Mexico. Nobody yet knows how it finds its way. It is one of the greatest of all insect travelers.

## HOW CAN AN INSECT HELP YOU TELL TEMPERATURE?

If you listen to a cricket chirping, you can guess the temperature outdoors. The warmer the day, the faster the song. One kind, the snowy tree cricket, sings the same musical note over and over. Count the number of times it sings in fifteen seconds. Then add forty. The resulting number will approximate the reading on a thermometer.

## ARE INSECTS HELPFUL TO US?

Although many insects eat our gardens and forests, some kinds are useful to us. Perhaps you have watched a pair of burying beetles as they dug under a dead mouse until it sank into the ground out of sight. Maybe you have seen ants cleaning up some garbage by taking it into their nest. One kind even carries away cigarette butts.

Ladybird beetles eat plant lice. Some kinds of stinkbugs feed on harmful caterpillars. Water striders keep the water clean by feeding on insects which drop from the bushes. Hornets fly around cows and horses, chasing the flies until they catch one for food.

Perhaps you have seen a painter using shellac. It looks like varnish and is used on boats and airplanes. It comes from the lac insect of India. Some brightly colored dyes are also made from insects. Silk is made by silkworms to cover their cocoons. The Chinese keep singing crickets in little cages. The groundup bodies of some insects are made into medicine.

## WHY DO BEES VISIT FLOWERS?

The drop of liquid found in the bottom of a flower is used by the bees in making honey. When the beekeeper takes the honeycomb from the hive, he always leaves plenty for the bees to eat during the winter. Otherwise they would starve. When bees go from one flower to another for the sweet nectar they make into food, they also pick up some pollen on the hairs of their body and legs. A little of this pollen brushes off as they visit each new flower. It helps the flowers' seeds and fruit to grow. Without bees, plants couldn't produce apples, peaches, melons and other good things we have to eat.

Fireflies in a cage make a useful "insect lantern" for the natives of some tropical lands.

## HOW ARE INSECTS
## USED IN LANTERNS?

When the natives in some tropical countries want to see after dark, they go outdoors with a little cage. They put a few fireflies in the cage. Each firefly has a spot in its body which glows when air is let in through the insect's air tubes. The shining of a dozen large fireflies helps brighten up the room. Some native girls even wear a firefly in their hair.

## WHICH INSECT IS WHICH?

Do you know the difference between a fly and a bee? Can you tell a moth from a butterfly? Are termites really white ants? You can have lots of fun learning to tell the insects apart. There are about two dozen different groups of insects. Each group is called an "order." The common insects belong to about eight orders. The following discussion will help you to know more about the kinds of insects you find and the groups to which they belong.

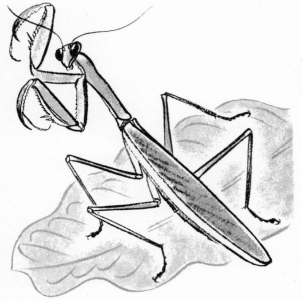

A praying mantis sits upon a leaf that it will soon eat.

## WHAT IS THE GRASSHOPPER FAMILY LIKE?

The praying mantis is the terror of the insect world. It catches and eats nearly every kind of insect it can find. It belongs in this group. The walking stick is also a relative of the grasshoppers. So are the cockroaches. Walking sticks eat plant leaves and twigs, but cockroaches eat nearly anything. Cockroaches have even eaten the glue from the backs of postage stamps.

Crickets and grasshoppers are the most musical of insects. They make most of the insect sounds you hear in the country. The mole cricket even sings under the ground. Locusts buzz their wings together as they fly, and katydids call from the treetops at night.

## ARE THE DRAGONFLY FAMILY REALLY "DARNING NEEDLES"?

People used to think dragonflies would sew up your ears while you were asleep. They called them "darning needles." Of course, they don't do any such thing. They are really helpful insects, for they catch thousands of mosquitoes. If you catch a dragonfly, notice its large eyes and funny legs. The eyes help it to see in almost every direction. The legs form a basket to catch other insects as it flies along. With its wings pointed out to the side, it looks like a small airplane.

Damselflies look like dragonflies and belong to this group. They fold their wings and point them up in the air. The nymphs of some dragonflies can travel by jet propulsion. They squirt water out of the end of their bodies. This makes them shoot forward like a little jet airplane. Perhaps it's more like a submarine, though, for they live under the water.

# WHAT ARE TERMITES?

Sometimes termites are called "white ants," but they are really not ants at all. Ants have a thin waist between the thorax and abdomen. Termites are thick-bodied from head to tail. Soldier termites guard the nest from enemies with their powerful jaws. Hundreds of workers build the nest and get the food. The queen lays great numbers of eggs. Sometimes there may be more than one queen, and a few kings as well.

Sometimes you see termites by the thousands as they come out on a window sill or old stump. These are dark-colored kings and queens ready to leave the nest. They fly to a new spot and then do a strange thing. They break off their wings so they can never fly again. Then they burrow into the ground and start a new colony.

Termites eat nearly everything made out of wood, leaving only a thin outer layer. Once a teacher opened an old desk drawer. Termites had drilled up through the floor and into the desk leg. They had hollowed out the wood of the desk until was just a shell. When he pulled on the drawer, the desk toppled.

A termite family in its nest. At top left, a winged reproductive and the queen with a soldier at her side. On the right, the king with workers behind him.

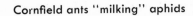
Cornfield ants "milking" aphids

## ARE ALL INSECTS "BUGS"?

The only real bugs are those with the soda-straw mouths made for poking into plants or drinking the blood of animals. Bugs have four wings or no wings at all. Half of the wing is tough, like a beetle's The other half is thin, like that of a fly. Squash bugs, bedbugs and stinkbugs are all true bugs. So is the diving water boatman with its long legs, which look like oars. Ladybugs and June bugs are not really bugs at all. They are beetles with chewing mouths.

The noisy cicada is a relative of the bugs. So are the green aphids. Aphids are interesting because they give off sweet honeydew which ants love. Some ants even carry aphids down into the ground to feed on the roots of plants. Then they have a honeydew supply right in the nest. This is almost like a farmer who keeps cows for milk. So we may say that ants keep aphids as "cows."

## WHAT IS THE BEETLE FAMILY LIKE?

There are more kinds of beetles than any other insect group in the world. If you began collecting beetles at the rate of one new kind every day, your life wouldn't be long enough to collect all of them. It would take seven hundred years. There are more than 250,000 known kinds. Sprinkle some salt in your hand. There are beetles so small that they could hide beneath a single grain of salt! There are beetles so large that when they spread their legs they would cover half this page! One of the largest of all insects is the Goliath beetle. It has a body almost as long as a banana. In fact, when a living specimen was sent to a museum, scientists found that it likes to eat bananas.

You can usually identify a beetle easily when you see it. It has powerful jaws for chewing. Heavy wings look like two shields on its back. Underneath are the folded wings which are used in flying. The wings of the Goliath beetle may spread eight inches. Stag beetles have jaws so large they look like the antlers of a tiny deer. Ground beetles have powerful jaws for eating other insects. The jaws of the boll weevil are out at the end of a long snout. It looks like a true bug at first, but if you look close you'll see its jaws.

(Above): Close-up of the head of a male stag beetle.

(Right): Stag beetles, male (top) and female (bottom).

## WHAT ARE THE DIFFERENCES BETWEEN MOTHS AND BUTTERFLIES?

Look at the way a moth holds its wings. The wings lie down flat over the moth's sides and back. A butterfly holds them pointed up over its back. Moths have antennae which look like feathers. The antennae of a butterfly look like long threads with a knot at the end. And, of course, you usually see moths at night and butterflies during the day.

Rub your finger gently on the wing of a butterfly or moth. You will find that a soft powder comes off. A microscope would show you that this powder is really thousands of tiny scales. They are arranged on the wing like shingles on a roof.

Some moths are not much larger than a pinhead. The largest may have a wingspan of more than a foot. Some are the most colorful of all insects. They may shine bright blue in one light, green or purple in another. These insects have a coiled tube for sipping liquids instead of the pointed beak of the bugs or the jaws of the beetles. They poke this tube down into flowers to get the sweet nectar.

Some moths are helpful to man. We unwind the silk from the silk-worm's cocoon. Many caterpillars eat troublesome weeds. But many butterflies and moths have babies which are not so helpful. They eat our gardens, our clothes and our forests.

## ARE MOTHS AND BUTTERFLIES DIFFERENT FROM OTHER INSECTS?

Moths and butterflies are divided into many smaller groups, or families. You can tell the families apart by their wing-veins, colors, and habits. It is not possible to list all the families and their members, but a few of the ones you may meet are mentioned here. There are other strange things about moths and butterflies. Like all insects they have no bones inside their bodies, which are protected by an outer jacket or *exo-skeleton*. Although they have a heart, there are no true arteries or veins. Blood, not red but green, yellow or colorless, flows through their hollow bodies and legs. Some butterflies have taste buds on their feet, so they can sample flowers they alight upon. Others have ears on their sides instead of on their heads. Sphinx moths sometimes squeak like a mouse when caught. A few caterpillars make a noise by grinding their jaws.

## WHAT ARE SOME OF THE FAMILIES OF MOTHS AND BUTTERFLIES?

BAGWORM MOTHS, *Psychidae (SIK-i-dee)*. Their silken pouches, covered with twigs or evergreen needles, are sometimes very common on trees and shrubs. The pouch looks almost like a little pine cone moving slowly along the tree branches.

BLUES, COPPERS AND HAIRSTREAKS, *Lycaenidae (Ly-SEN-i-dee)*. These are very small butterflies. Although often brown in color, they may have a beautiful blue glint to their wings. Some of the larvae of the blues feed on other insects. The hairstreaks and coppers belong to the same family.

BRUSH-FOOTED BUTTERFLIES, *Nymphalidae (Nim-FAL-i-dee)*. This large family has front legs which look like little brushes. They usually walk with just the last two pair of legs. The family includes the mourning cloak, fritillaries, tortoise-shells, and admirals.

CLEAR-WING MOTHS, *Aegeriidae (e-JER-i-dee)*. With few scales on their wings, they look like bees or wasps. Some are colored yellow and black, and may even pretend to sting. Their larvae are borers in peach trees and other kinds of plants.

CLOTHES MOTHS, *Tineidae (Ti-NEE-i-dee)*. Tiny clothes moths, no bigger than a fly, sometimes burst out of a closet when it is opened. Their numerous larvae feed on wool and fur. It is for protection against them that "moth crystals" are made.

CODLING MOTHS, *Pyralidae (Pi-RAL-i-dee)*. If you have ever bitten into a wormy apple, you have probably met the larva of the codling moth. The adult is a little brown moth which flies around lights in summer. The Mexican jumping bean larva is in this family. The European corn borer, aquatic caterpillars, and the little wax moth of beehives are relatives of codling moths.

MEASURING-WORM MOTHS, *Geometridae (JEE-a-MET-ri-dee)*. Inchworms, loopers, and measuring-worms are all larvae of this family. The adults,

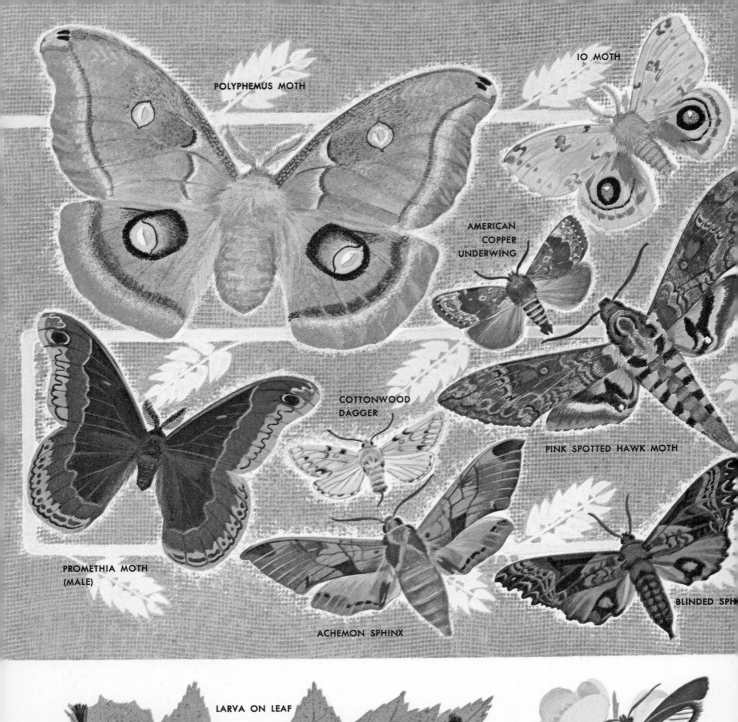

POLYPHEMUS MOTH

IO MOTH

AMERICAN COPPER UNDERWING

COTTONWOOD DAGGER

PINK SPOTTED HAWK MOTH

PROMETHIA MOTH (MALE)

ACHEMON SPHINX

BLINDED SPH

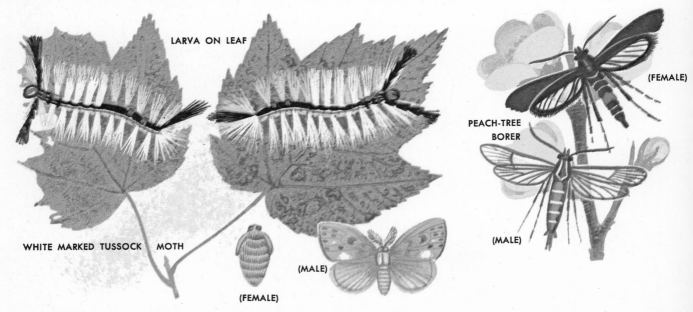

LARVA ON LEAF

WHITE MARKED TUSSOCK MOTH

(FEMALE)

(MALE)

PEACH-TREE BORER

(FEMALE)

(MALE)

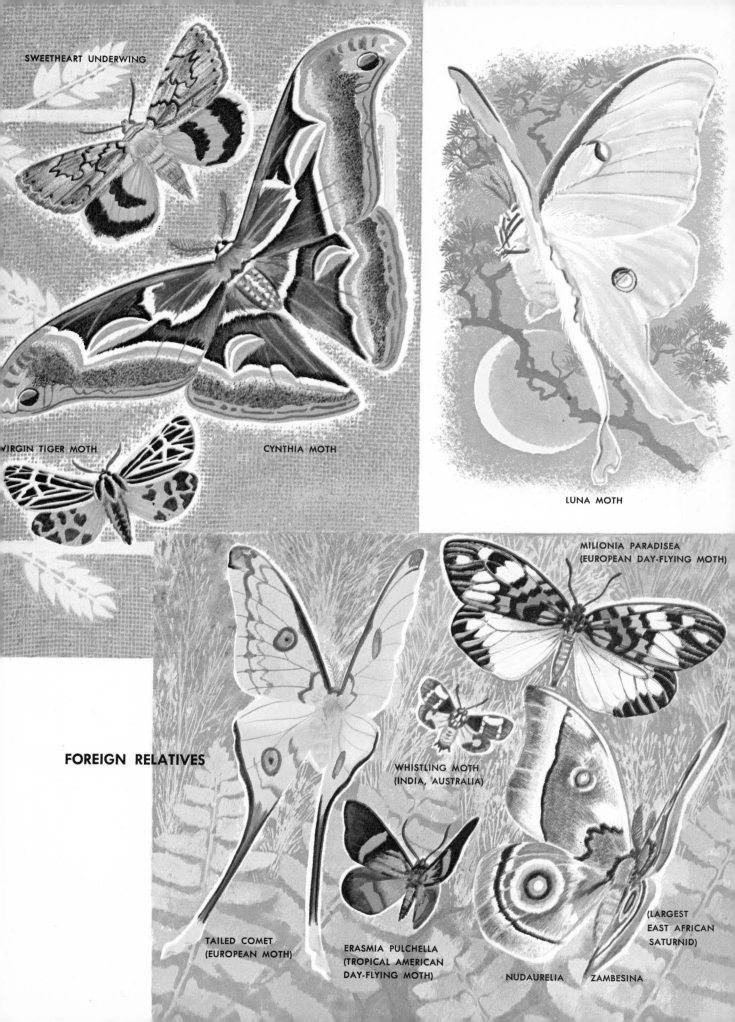

SWEETHEART UNDERWING

VIRGIN TIGER MOTH

CYNTHIA MOTH

LUNA MOTH

MILIONIA PARADISEA
(EUROPEAN DAY-FLYING MOTH)

WHISTLING MOTH
(INDIA, AUSTRALIA)

**FOREIGN RELATIVES**

TAILED COMET
(EUROPEAN MOTH)

ERASMIA PULCHELLA
(TROPICAL AMERICAN
DAY-FLYING MOTH)

NUDAURELIA    ZAMBESINA

(LARGEST
EAST AFRICAN
SATURNID)

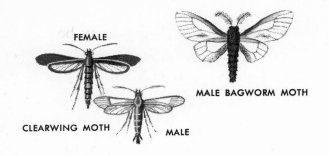

FEMALE

MALE BAGWORM MOTH

CLEARWING MOTH

MALE

ADULT

LARVA

EUROPEAN CORNBORER

FEMALE

MALE

FALL CANKERWORM

LARVA

CORN EARWORM

dainty like butterflies, have delicate markings on the light-colored wings.

MONARCH BUTTERFLIES, *Danaidae (Da-*NAY-*i-dee)*. The familiar orange and black monarch butterfly and its relatives are found over most of the world. It is known for its long migrations. The queen, also in this family, is chocolate brown and black.

OWL MOTHS, *Noctuidae (Nok-*TU-*i-dee)*. This is the largest family of Lepidoptera, found all over the world, and characterized by their dusky tints and nocturnal habits. Cutworm moths, in this family, often feed on plants. The caterpillars of the cotton worm moth destroy the bolls on cotton plants.

SILKWORM MOTHS, *Saturniidae (Sat-*UHRN-*i-dee)*. Here are the giant cecropia, polyphemus, and luna moth. Most of these moths are large, furry, and have beautiful colors. The silkworm is also found in this family. Its moth is small and light-colored.

SKIPPERS, *Hesperiidae (Hes-*PER-*i-dee)*. Fast-flying little insects, the skippers look almost like a cross between butterflies and moths. Many skippers have a fringe of hair which looks like eyelashes above their compound eyes. Skipper larvae have a small neck which looks as if they were wearing a tight-fitting collar.

SPHINX or HAWK MOTHS, *Sphingi-dae (*SFIN-*geh-dee)*. These large, narrow-winged moths are streamlined for swift flight. The front wings may be beautifully marked in black, brown, and white. The hind wings may be pink, yellow, or several colors. Tomato hornworms are sphinx larvae.

SWALLOWTAIL BUTTERFLIES AND PARNASSIANS, *Papilionidae (Pap-PIL-yon-i-dee)*. The swallowtails are a common sight in the country. They have two long "tails" like those of a barn swallow.

TIGER MOTHS, *Arctiidae (Ark-TEH-i-dee)*. These small moths may be beautifully marked like a tiger. They are not ferocious, however, but are named because of their color. The woolly bear caterpillar is a tiger moth larva.

WHITES AND SULPHUR BUTTERFLIES, *Pieridae (Pe-ER-i-dee)*. This family includes the little sulphur and cabbage butterflies. Most of these are yellow or white. The dog face butterfly has a picture of a dog on its wings.

# WHAT IS THE FLY FAMILY LIKE?

When you catch a fly or mosquito, count its wings. The total may surprise you. All the other common insects have four wings, but the flies have only two. Instead of a second pair, they have a pair of knobs attached to the thorax. If these knobs are hurt, they cannot fly.

One of the strangest flies lives in the fur of some animals. It has no wings, and runs around in the hair of sheep, goats and deer. It looks like a big flea. A few other wingless flies live in the feathers of some birds. Still another, a wingless crane fly, can sometimes be seen walking around on the snow. It looks like a spider, but has only six legs instead of the spider's eight. It is one of the first insects to come out in the spring.

A few tropical flies are among the most dangerous of all insects. The anopheles mosquito carries malaria disease from one person to another. The aedes mosquito carries yellow fever. The tsetse flies of Africa carry sleeping sickness. Houseflies may go right from a garbage pail to your dinner table. Doctors worked many years before they found ways to control these insects. Many of them caught the same diseases they were fighting.

Some flies look like other insects. Some are colored exactly like a bee. Others look like wasps or hornets. Some look like moths. But if you count the wings, you'll see that they are not wasps and bees at all — they are flies.

# HOW DO YOU TELL AN ANT, BEE OR WASP FROM OTHER INSECTS?

If you see an insect with a slender waist, the chances are that it is an ant, bee or wasp. If it has four clear-colored wings, you can be almost certain of it. Some flies and moths look like them, but flies have only two wings and moths have thick bodies. Many of these insects live in large nests, so they are called "social insects." There is a queen that lays the eggs. She is cared for by the workers. They bring food and enlarge the nest for more new babies. All of the workers are females. Sometimes the queen lays eggs which hatch into males. The males fly from the nest and mate with new queens. Then the queens start new nests of their own.

## WHAT HAPPENS INSIDE THE HIVE?

Inside the hive is an amazing scene. No factory ever ran with more bustle and activity. Hanging from the roof are heavy curtains of wax.

A blind and legless grub hatches from the egg. It is fed continuously until it starts spinning a cocoon after a few days.

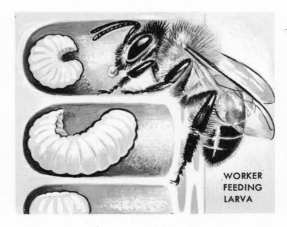

WORKER FEEDING LARVA

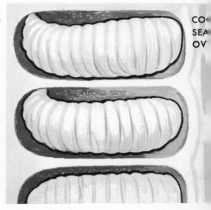

CO
SEA
OV

They may be larger than this book and four times as thick. On both sides of the curtains are countless honeybees, poking their heads into hundreds of little cells or chambers. This is the castle of ten thousand rooms. Each cell of the curtains is a little room by itself. Although we often speak of the curtains as "honeycomb," a great many of them do not contain honey at all. The cells of the brood comb each have a small inhabitant — a grublike larva that will soon turn into a new honeybee. For the larva, the cell is a cradle, living room and bedroom combined. The larva stays in it from the day it hatches until the day it is fully grown. Nurse bees are walking all over the brood comb. Sometimes they put their feet right on the heads of the babies. One after the other, they bend down and poke their heads inside the cells. They feed and lick their little sisters in their cradles.

There is another kind of cell on the edge of the comb. It is much larger than the others. It looks almost like a peanut shell made out of wax. Inside it is a larva just like the thousands of others — only a little larger. This strange cell must be something special to be off on the side of the comb where it can have plenty of room. Indeed it is, for it is the royal nursery of the larva that will soon become the new queen. Over on the true "honeycomb," something strange is taking place. Bees are walking slowly over the half-filled cells, beating their wings as if they were trying to fly. As the breeze from their wings fans across the cells, it makes the sweet liquid evaporate. A cell that was filled with honey may be only three-quarters full the next day as a result of the air from their wings. This seems like a waste — to bring in nectar from the flowers and then evaporate it so there is not much left. But one taste of the liquid will tell why it is done. The sugar that stays behind as the water evaporates gets thicker and sweeter.

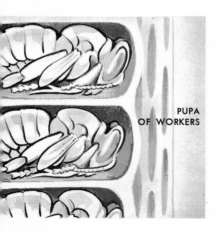

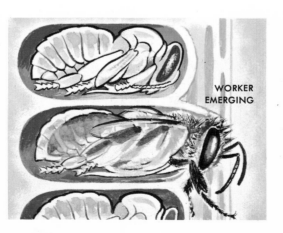

PUPA OF WORKERS

WORKER EMERGING

Here, in the cocoon, the great change takes place: from grub to milk-white nymph or pupa, until one day the adult bee emerges. If the egg is fertilized, the bee will become a worker. If not fertilized, it will become a drone.

# WHY ARE BEES IMPORTANT TO FLOWERS AND PLANTS?

Mixed from flower to flower, pollen is needed for blossoms to develop their fruit and seeds. The seeds can grow into new plants. If the bees didn't scatter the pollen, there would probably be no orchards. Apples, peaches, strawberries, oranges and other fruit would be unknown. There would be no pretty flowers in the garden. The honey produced by bees in the United States alone is worth about a hundred million dollars each year. This, however, is small compared to the value of all the fruit and flowers.

Why doesn't the pollen from a dandelion get mixed with the flower from a rose? Simply because the honeybee visits only one kind of flower at a time. She may fly over a whole field of dandelions to get to a rose garden. The next day, she may visit nothing but clover.

# HOW DO BEES TELL EACH OTHER WHERE THE NECTAR IS?

An apple tree begins to unfold its flowers early one May morning. By eight o'clock, hundreds of fragrant pink-and-white blooms have opened. A single bee discovers them. She takes nectar from a few blossoms. Then she stuffs her baskets with pollen, circles around for a few seconds and is gone. In less than half an hour the tree is buzzing with dozens of honeybees. How did she tell them about her wonderful find of a tree full of flowers?

The answer was found by Dr. Karl von Frisch of Germany, when he discovered the "dancing bees." When the worker returned from the apple tree, she began to do a little dance near the entrance to the hive. First she circled one way, then another. In between the circles she walked a little straight line, wiggling like an excited puppy. Soon the others followed her in her dance, doing just the same as she was doing. The circles tell how far away the flowers are — the more circles, the farther away. The straight line tells the direction to travel, and the odor of the flowers still clinging to her body tells them what kind of flowers they will find. In a few minutes they fly away, one after another — right to the apple tree!

The more circles a bee "dances," the farther away are flowers with nectar.

The straight line in the bee's dance shows the direction of the flower. The tail-wagging gives the scent.

## HOW DO BEES TELL DIRECTIONS?

Beekeepers know that bees find their way by means of the sun. But what do they do on a cloudy day? They can still sense where the sun is in the sky by means of polarized light. This is light that can be seen better from one direction than from others. Even behind the clouds, the sun still sends it down. Ultraviolet light, too — the same invisible rays that cause a sunburn — guides the bees. And their huge compound eyes make out the shape of familiar trees and houses. They find their way by the color of flowers, too — all but one color. The bees are color-blind to red.

## HOW LONG DO BEES LIVE?

Day after day the bee travels back and forth. Little hooks between her wings hold them together for strength in flight. The wings buzz as much as two hundred times per second. But in a few days they begin to get frayed on the edges. In a couple of weeks they are slightly torn. A little more than a month from the time she first spread their shining beauty in the sun, the faithful wings are tattered She works with them until she can fly no longer. One day she finds her load of pollen and nectar too heavy. The bee drops to the ground, half-crawling, half-flying toward the hive. There, six or eight weeks after she visited her first flower, her days of work come to an end.

## DO ALL BEES LIVE IN HIVES?

Carpenter bees dig holes in wood. Bumblebees make their home in holes in the ground. Sometimes they use an old mouse nest. They almost seem to be paying the mice back for living in the hives of honeybees. Mason bees lay their eggs in an old snail shell or knothole. A mason bee might even use a keyhole in a door for its home, cementing it shut with sand and clay.

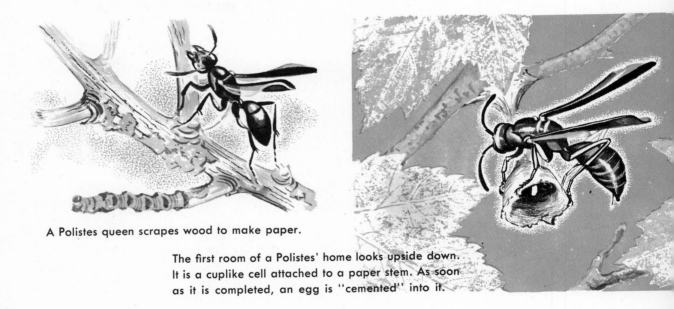

A Polistes queen scrapes wood to make paper.

The first room of a Polistes' home looks upside down. It is a cuplike cell attached to a paper stem. As soon as it is completed, an egg is "cemented" into it.

## HOW DO WASPS AND HORNETS MAKE PAPER?

Wasps and hornets were the first paper makers. Long before humans learned to grind wood into paper, these insects were chewing bits of sticks, which they then mixed with saliva from their mouths. They shaped this material into nests. When it dried, they had a strong paper house in which to live. Some wasps hunt and kill spiders. Others catch harmful caterpillars. Some of the smallest wasps thrust their eggs into the bodies of our garden pests. Then the tiny babies bore through the insect and kill it. They may be no larger than the size of the period at the end of this sentence.

## HOW DO ANTS LIVE?

Many ants are peaceful farmers or explorers. The terrible driver ants, however, eat everything in their path. Sometimes they enter jungle huts, and the natives flee for their lives. The driver ants chase away or kill every mouse and rat, insect and spider.

Like the swarming bees or the paperwasps in the fall, the ants lay aside their daily work. Workers and soldiers rush back and forth. They wave their antennae and push each other. Sometimes a huge soldier picks up a little worker and carriers her around for half an hour. In the middle of it all the queens and drones flutter their untried wings. The activity spills outside the nest, like boiling water from a kettle. One after the other the winged ones climb up sticks and blades of grass. They stretch their new wings for a moment — and are gone. Up into the air they go, until they are tiny points of light in the sunshine. They have left the nest forever. The wingless workers that have followed them to the tips of the grass blades now turn back toward the ant hill below. All around are the chattering birds. Robber flies and dragonflies dart back and forth. Spiders find their webs filled with dozens of new victims. The whole meadow is filled with activity, for hundreds of nests have sent out their little aviators at once. Now the birds and other creatures are having a feast.

This cross section through the nest of the garden ants shows the mound of earth thrown up by the insects. Passages lead deep into the ground where the real nest lies.

# WHAT DO ANTS EAT?

While bees eat only nectar and pollen, ants eat many things. They eat nectar if they can get it, but pollen is too hard for their taste. They eat insects and the sweet juices of fruit. Seeds of grasses and berries are also a part of their diet. When an ant comes across a large supply of food, it rushes back to the nest. Waving its antennae and striking with its feet, it whacks every ant in its path. It pushes them away from whatever they are doing. Such unusual behavior sets them to doing the same thing, until they are all jostling and shoving. Sometimes they even butt each other with their heads, like little goats. Soon the nest looks as if it were a free-for-all fight. Now they begin to spill out of the nest, still pushing and shoving. They run around in little circles and zigzag lines. Sooner or later a few find the food. Then the pushing starts all over again as soon as they get back home. This may keep up until the food is gone. Sometimes several ants find a chunk of food at once, and try to bring it back to the nest. Most of them pull in the right direction, but a few do not. They tug north while the rest tug south. Some even get on top and tug upward!

# ARE THERE PLANTS THAT FEED ON INSECTS?

A few plants feed on insects. They are called insectivorous plants. The pitcher plant has leaves which are hollow and shaped like a flower vase. Rain water falls into them and makes a little puddle. Insects fall into the water and drown. Then the plant digest the insects, somewhat as you digest the food you eat. Some pitcher plants are so large that they may trap frogs, lizards or even mice. The sundew has sticky hairs on its leaves. Insects land on the leaves and get tangled in the sticky surface. Soon, like those in the pitcher plant, they are digested. The milkweed catches insects, but it lets them go again. It has flowers with little traps in them. When an insect puts its foot in the trap, it is held fast. Then it struggles to get free. Finally the trap breaks off, and the insect flies away with it. Then when it visits another milkweed, grains of pollen in the trap fall out on the new blossom, so the milkweed can make its seeds.

Some plants even live inside the bodies of insects. One fungus attacks houseflies and kills them. Another kind attacks caterpillars. Bacteria, which are so small that you need a microscope to see them, kill many others. Without these little plants, there would be even more insects in the world than there are now.

## DO SOME INSECTS LIVE IN PLANTS?

Many kinds of insects cause galls on plants. Some are made by flies. The mother fly lays her eggs in the stem of a plant. The stem begins to swell. The eggs hatch inside the swelling. Then the maggots live in their strange house. Insects are useful in carrying seeds of plants. Small hooks on the seeds may catch in the hairs on the body of a fly or bee. Then the seed is carried through the air as the insect flies away. Later it drops off and starts a new plant. Some insects take seeds to their nests in the ground. The seeds may grow, starting a new plant right in the middle of the nest.

## WHAT IS THE MEXICAN JUMPING BEAN?

This is a seed which contains a small caterpillar. This little insect chews away at the inside of the seed. It changes position every few minutes. Every time it moves, the seed rolls around, just as you can roll a big box by moving around inside it. Finally the caterpillar turns into a little moth. Then it flies away to lay its eggs in new seeds.

## WHAT ARE FOSSIL INSECTS?

If an insect, usually a large one, lands in soft mud or clay, it may get stuck there and eventually die. Frequently, the insect becomes completely buried in the mud, which may later turn into rock. When the insect wastes away, it leaves a natural print, or mold, of its body. Then, when the rock is broken, a picture-outline of the insect may be seen. Such prints and molds are known as "fossils."

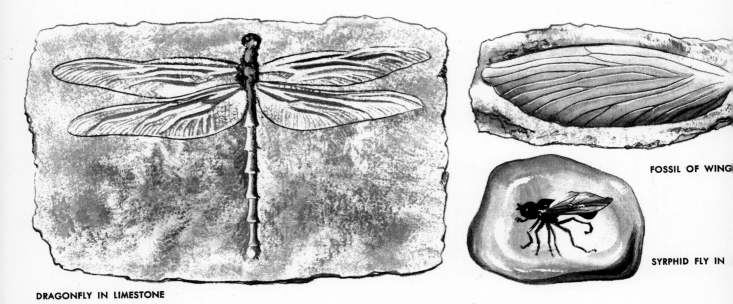

FOSSIL OF WING

SYRPHID FLY IN

DRAGONFLY IN LIMESTONE

One of the most interesting insect fossils is the "amber fossil." Many kinds of trees, such as pines and spruces, have a sticky material known as resin. You may find it on the bark and trunk. Flies, ants, wasps and other insects often get tangled in this resin. More of it flows over them, covering them with a clear coating. Later this resin changes and hardens, becoming a substance known as amber. If there are insects inside, they will be preserved for millions of years by the hard material.

No one can be sure just when the first insects lived on this earth. Scientists have found insect fossils about 240 million years old. Some day they may find some that are still older. It is as interesting to hunt for fossil insects as it is to collect modern ones.

## WHAT IS NEEDED TO COLLECT INSECTS?

You will need these things:

(1) A magnifying glass.

(2) A pair of tweezers.

(3) A few dozen pins. (Regular insect pins are best. Perhaps a biology teacher can help you get some. If not, you may have to use common pins.)

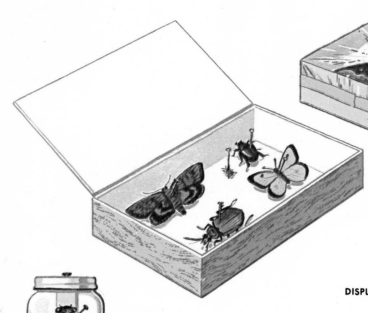

DISPLAY BOXES

DISPLAY MOUNT

DISPLAY JARS

MOUNTING BOARD

KILLING JAR

MAGNIFYING GLASS

(4) A box with a tight cover, such as a cigar box or a candy box.

(5) A piece of thick cardboard, cut to fit exactly into the bottom of the box. (With this, pins may be stuck in easily.)

(6) A killing jar. (This should have a tight lid. A pint-size jar will be fine. Put a crumpled piece of paper towel in the bottom, wet it with a few drops of cleaning fluid and force a circle of cardboard into the jar a little above the paper so that the insect cannot touch the damp paper. Keep the jar tightly closed when you are not using it.)

## HOW DO I PREPARE AN INSECT?

After you catch an insect, put it in the bottle for five minutes. It will quiet down right away. When it is still, take it out with the tweezers. To keep your insect in good condition, carefully stick a pin through its thorax or chest from the top. Push the pin down until the pinhead is about one quarter of an inch above the insect's back. Beetles should have the pin stuck through the right wing. Put a small label on the pin, telling where and when you found the insect. If you know its name, put this on another label.

Stick the pin into the soft cardboard bottom of the box, and you'll be able to look at the insect whenever you wish. Always handle it with care after it is dry. You can mount tiny insects, too. Glue them to one

corner of a three-cornered piece of paper. Then push your pin through the center of the paper. Butterflies and moths should have the wings spread. Do this as soon as possible after collecting them. Don't let them dry out. Spread the wings flat on a piece of soft wood, one at a time, until all four wings are out straight. Hold them in place with strips of waxed paper. Never put pins through the wings.

# HOW DO I PRESERVE AN INSECT?

If an insect gets hard and dry, it can be relaxed and softened with steam from an iron. Place it in a saucer and let the steam from the iron point right at the insect. Or put it on a piece of wire screen over hot water. In a few minutes you can handle the insect without breaking it.

Put a few moth crystals in the box every three months. These are the same crystals used to protect winter clothing when it is stored away in the spring. Then other insects won't get in and eat up your collection. You can also keep insects in tiny bottles of alcohol. Regular rubbing alcohol is good. Their colors soon fade, but insects will stay soft.

# CAN LIVING INSECTS BE KEPT?

You can make a little home for living insects. Then you can watch them grow and eat. Put some sand and twigs in a large glass jar. Put a small pill bottle filled with water in the sand. Then you can put leaves in the jar and the leaves will not dry up. If you are raising a caterpillar, be sure you feed it plenty of the right kind of leaves. Use a good big jar, so that it will have plenty of room to spread its wings later.

You can make a little insect aquarium. Fill a goldfish bowl half full of water. Put in a few pebbles and weeds for hiding places. Keep it out of bright light or the water will turn green. Then you can put any water insect in your aquarium. Cover the top, because most water insects can fly. Your pets will feed on a bit of liver or fish. Serve it to them on a pair of tweezers, or hang it in the water by thread. Take out, in an hour, all food that they don't eat. In that way, decaying food will not foul the water.

You can find insect eggs and cocoons on twigs and dead leaves in winter. Keep them on the outside window sill until you are ready for them to hatch. The cold air will keep them fresh and healthy. If you keep them indoors where it is warm, they may hatch too soon.

WOOD

TAPE

GLASS

EYE DROPPER

FOOD

WATER

A formicarium with earth between the panes of glass offers a good opportunity to study the interesting life of ants.

## HOW DO I MAKE A HOME FOR ANTS?

An observation ant home is called a *formicarium*. It can be made of two panes of glass separated by strips of wood around the edges. Then, if a small ant hill is dug up carefully, you will find the humpbacked queen. Put her in a jar with some of her workers, larvae and cocoons. You will probably discover that you have some of the strange ant guests, too. Carefully place them all in the formicarium.

No soil is needed for your ant nest. Before you seal it up, place a sponge near one edge for moisture. Drill two holes in the wood for two medicine droppers. One is to wet the sponge, and the other is for honey, water and melted butter with a little egg white. This will serve as food for the ants. Then the panes are taped together. Keep the nest covered with dark paper except when looking at the ants.

# WHAT ABOUT DISPLAYING AN INSECT COLLECTION?

You can make a fine display with your insect collection. Beetles, grasshoppers and dragonflies can be mounted in special boxes and then hung on the wall of your room. Mounted butterflies and moths make interesting "pictures" to hang on walls or to give as gifts.

To make a display case, find a large flat box, such as a writing paper box or candy box. Measure it and cut a piece of glass so that it will just fit over the box. Glue a picture hanger on the back of the box so it can be hung up later. Fill the box with cotton. It is a good idea to put some moth crystals in the cotton as protection against other insects.

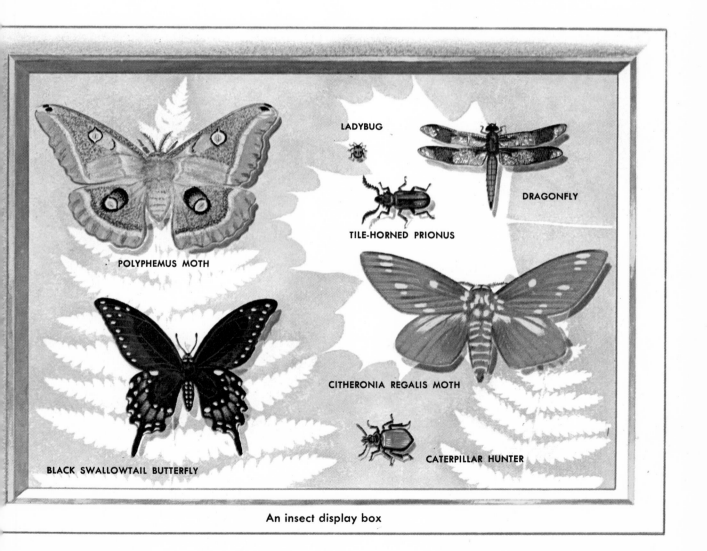

An insect display box

Place your insects carefully on the cotton. Press them down so they will stay in place. Butterflies and moths should be mounted while they are still soft and flexible. Then put the glass plate over them and seal it neatly around the edges with tape. A coat of black enamel over the box and the tape will seal all the small holes and make a good-looking display case.

Some companies make black cases with white cotton just for insects. These are called Riker mounts. A biology teacher will be able to tell you where you can get them. The teacher can also tell you about special kits for mounting insects in a dish of liquid plastic. When the plastic hardens, you can take it out of the dish like an ice cube. Then it can be used as an ornament for your desk or as a gift.

## IS A MAGNIFYING GLASS USEFUL?

A magnifying glass will help you learn much more about insects. It will show you many things too small to see without a lens. You may find an extra pair of eyes on the whirligig beetle, for instance. One is for seeing in the air, while the other is for looking under water. If you look in the center of a daisy, you'll see tiny black thrips. A close look at their legs shows that they walk around with feet that look like little balloons. Treehoppers look like prehistoric dinosaurs when they are seen under the magnifying glass.

In a few years, space ships may take men to Mars. They may even go beyond our own solar system. Some experts think they'll find strange new forms of life. But with a magnifying glass and a good sharp eye, we can stay home and find strange creatures of our own. Few animals that have ever lived are much stranger than the flies and beetles and bugs that live in the world right at our fingertips.

# INDEX

Numerals in *italics*
refer to pictures.

## A

achemon sphinx, *40*
admirals, 39
aedes mosquito, 43
*Aegeriidae,* 39
"amber fossil," 51-52
American copper underwing, *40*
anopheles mosquito, 43
ant lion, *22, 23*
ants, 10, 11, 16, 22, 23, 32, 35, 52
  eating habits of, 50
  living habits of, 49
  nest of garden ants, *49—see also* specific names
aphids, green, 36
aquatic caterpillars, 39

## B

bagworm moth (*Psychidae*), 39
  male, *42*
bedbug, 36
beehive, 31, 44
bees, 10, 22, 31, 32, 33, 43, 46, 47, 50, 51
  "dancing bees," 46
  development from cocoon to adult, 44-45
  larva of, 45
  life span of, 48—see also specific names
beetles, 9, 10, 16, 19, 20, 23, 57
  collecting, preparation for, 54—*see also* specific names
bird dust bath, *12, 14*
black swallowtail butterfly, *57*
blinded sphinx, *40*
brush-footed butterflies (*Nymphalidae*), 39
burrowing beetles, 10
burying beetles, 31
butterflies, 8, 9, 19, 28, *28,* 57, 58
  collecting, preparation for, 54—*see also* specific names
bumblebees, 19, 48
bugs, 36
boll weevil, 37

## C

cabbage butterflies, 43
  egg of, *17*
cadisfly larva, 22
carpenter bees, 48
cankerworm (fall), *42*
caterpillar, 16, 19, 20, 23, 29, 30, 32, 38, 49, 51
  body segments of, 26, *26*
  enemies of, 26-27
  molting, 27
  pupa of, 28—*see also* specific names
centipede, *8*
cicada, 14, 17-18, 36
Citheronia Regalis moth, *57*
clearwing moth, *42*
clothes moths, 18
clouded locust, 25
cloudless sulphur, *25*
cockroach, nymph of, 30, 34
coddling moths, larva of, *21,* 39
cornborer, European, *42*
corn earworm, *42*
cornfield ant, *36*

cottonworm moth, 42
cricket, 9, 10, 11, 14, 20, 31, 32, 34
cutworm moth, 42

## D

damselflies, 18, *19,* 34
*Danaidae* (monarch Butterflies), 30, 31, 39, 42
  eggs of, *17*
"dancing bees," 46, *47*
displaying insects, 57, *57*
diving beetles, 10
diving waterboatman, 36
dogface butterfly, 43
dragonflies (darning needles), 14, 18, *19,* 34, 49, *57*
  fossil of, *52*
driver ants, 49
dust bath, bird, *12, 14*

## E

European cornborer, 39

## F

facets, 14-15
fireflies, 33
fleas, 9, 30
flies, 10, 12, *13*
  eggs of, 16, 18, 19, 20, 30, 32, 33
  family of, 43-44
  maggots of, 51, 52—*see also* specific names
fossil insects, 51-52
froghopper fly, *22,* 23
formicarium, *56*
fritillaries, 39

## G

galls, insect, 11-12, *11,* 51
*Geometridae,* 39
goldenrod gall, *11*
Goliath beetle, 37
grasshopper, *12,* 14, 16, *18,* 19
  family of, 34
ground beetle, 37
grub, 19, 20, 29

## H

harlequin bug, egg of, *17*
hawk moths (sphinx), 42
honeybees, 45, 46, 48
Hornet moth, *24*
hornets, 32, 48
hornworms, tomato, 43
houseflies, 14, 43, 51

## I

ichneumon flies, 10
inchworms, 39, 42
insectivorous, 50
insects, 8, 12, 25, 51
  antennae, 15
  aquarium of, 55
  body structure of, 9, *9*
  breathing, 13-14
  collecting procedures for, 52-58
  communication among, 14
  display instructions for, 57-58
  eggs of, 16-18
  eggs and cocoons, collection of, 55
  eyes of, 14-15
  feeding, 20
  homes of babies, 22-23
  instincts of, 23
  kinds of, 10

materials for collecting, 52-54
  nature's protection of, 23-24
  orders of, 33-34
  pupa of, 28-30

## J

Japanese beetle, 23
junebug, 36

## K

katydid, 34
killing jars, *53*

## L

lac, 32
lacewing, egg, *17*
lacewing fly, 20
ladybird beetle, 32
ladybug, 36
larvae, 19
Lepidoptera, 42
lice, 30
  eggs of, 18
living insects, how to keep, 55
locust, 20, *21,* 34
luna moth, *41,* 42
Lycaenidae, 39

## M

maggot (fly), 9, 10, 19
magnifying glass, *53,* 58
mason bees, 48
measuring-worm moths (*Geometridae*), 39
Mexican Bean Beetles (and larvae), *21*
Mexican jumping bean, 51
  larva, 39
Milionia Paradisea, *41*
milkweed, 50
Millipede, *8*
mole cricket, 10, 34
monarch butterflies (*Danaidae*), 31, 42
  eggs of, *17*
mosquitos, 10, 12, 18, 34, 43
moths, 9, 14, 15, *18,* 19, 20, *24, 25, 28,* 33, 38, 39, *41-42,* 43-44, 58—*see also* specific names
mounting board, *53*
mourning cloak butterfly, 30, 39
  egg of, *17*

## N

*Noctuidae,* 42
*Nudaurelia, 41*
nurse bees, 45
*Nymphalidae,* 39
nymphs, 19

## O

oak gall wasp, *11*
owl moths (*Noctuidae*), 42

## P

paper makers, 49
*Papilionidae,* 43
Parnassians, 43
peach-tree borer, *40*
*Pieridae,* 43
pink spotted hawk moth, *40*
pitcher plant, 50
plant lice, 32
plants, insect eating, 50
polistes wasp, *48*
Polyphemus moth, *40, 57*
porcupine oak gall, *11*

potter wasp, *22*
praying mantis, 10, 17
  nymphs of, 30, 34, *34*
preserving insects, 55
Promethia moth, larva, *28*
  male, *40*
*Psychidae,* 39
*Pyralidae,* 39

## Q

queen bees, 45

## R

Riker mounts, 58
robber flies, 49

## S

*Saturniidae,* 42
scorpion fly, *21*
silk worm, 32, 38
  moths of, 42
singing crickets, 31, 32
skippers, 42
small oak gall, *11*
snowy tree cricket, 31
"social insects," 44
*Sphingidae,* 42
Sphinx moths, 39, 42
  larvae of, 43
spice-bush swallowtail caterpillar, *26*
spiders, 8, *8,* 9, 48, 49
spiracles, *12,* 13-14
springtail, 11
squash bug 23, nymph of, 30, 36
stag beetles, 37, *37*
stinkbug, 32, 36
sulphur butterflies, 43
sundew, 50
swallowtail butterflies, *8*
  eggs of, *17,* 43
swarming bees, 49
sweetheart underwing, *41*
syphid fly (fossil), *52*

## T

tailed comet (European moth), *41*
10 moth, *40*
tent caterpillar, eggs of, 16
termites, 16-17, 22, 33, 35, *35*
tiger beetle, 10
tiger moths, 43
tile-horned prionus, *57*
*Tineidae,* 39
tortoise-shells, 39
tsetse flies, 43

## V

Viceroy butterfly, *24*
virgin tiger moth, *41*

## W

walking stick, 10, 18
wasps, 10, 11
  parasitic egg of, *28,* 48, 52
  Polistes, *48*
water bug, 18, 25
water striders, 10
wax moth, 39
whirligig beetle, 58
whistling moth, *41*
white marked tussock, *40*
wingless crane fly, 43
woodborers, 20

## Z

Zambesina, *41*